Radical Rocks

by Rena Korb
illustrations by Brandon Reibeling

Content Consultant:
Daniel V. Sola • Professional Geologist, Wenck Associates

visit us at www.abdopublishing.com

Published by Magic Wagon, a division of the ABDO Publishing Group, 8000 West 78th Street, Edina, Minnesota, 55439.

Printed in the United States.

Text by Rena Korb
Illustrations by Brandon Reibeling
Edited by Nadia Higgins
Interior layout and design by Ryan Haugen
Cover design by Brandon Reibeling

Library of Congress Cataloging-in-Publication Data

Korb, Rena B.
Radical rocks / Rena Korb ; illustrated by Brandon Reibeling ; content consultant, Daniel V. Sola.
p. cm. — (Science rocks!)
ISBN 978-1-60270-040-6
1. Rocks—Juvenile literature. 2. Petrology—Juvenile literature. I. Reibeling, Brandon, ill. II. Title.
QE432.2.K67 2008
552—dc22

2007006333

Table of Contents

A World of Rocks

What is a rock?

Is it something you skip in a river?

Is it something you kick along a sidewalk?

Is it something you climb on just for fun?

A rock is all this and a whole lot more.

Earth is mostly made up of rocks. Water, soil, plants, and roads cover Earth's surface. If you dug far enough down, you'd hit solid rock.

Even towering mountains are really rocks!

Did you know there are space rocks? Some rocks got here when meteorites from outer space landed on Earth!

Colorful Minerals

Look closely at a slab of granite.
Do you see how it is speckled
gray, pink, and green?
Each of those colors comes
from a different mineral.

Minerals form in the earth.
They are the ingredients that
make up rocks.

Not all rocks are speckled. Often the grains of minerals inside a rock are really small. They're all mixed up together. You'd need a magnifying glass to see the different colors.

Three Types of Rocks

There are three groups of rocks: igneous, sedimentary, and metamorphic. These rocks form in different ways.

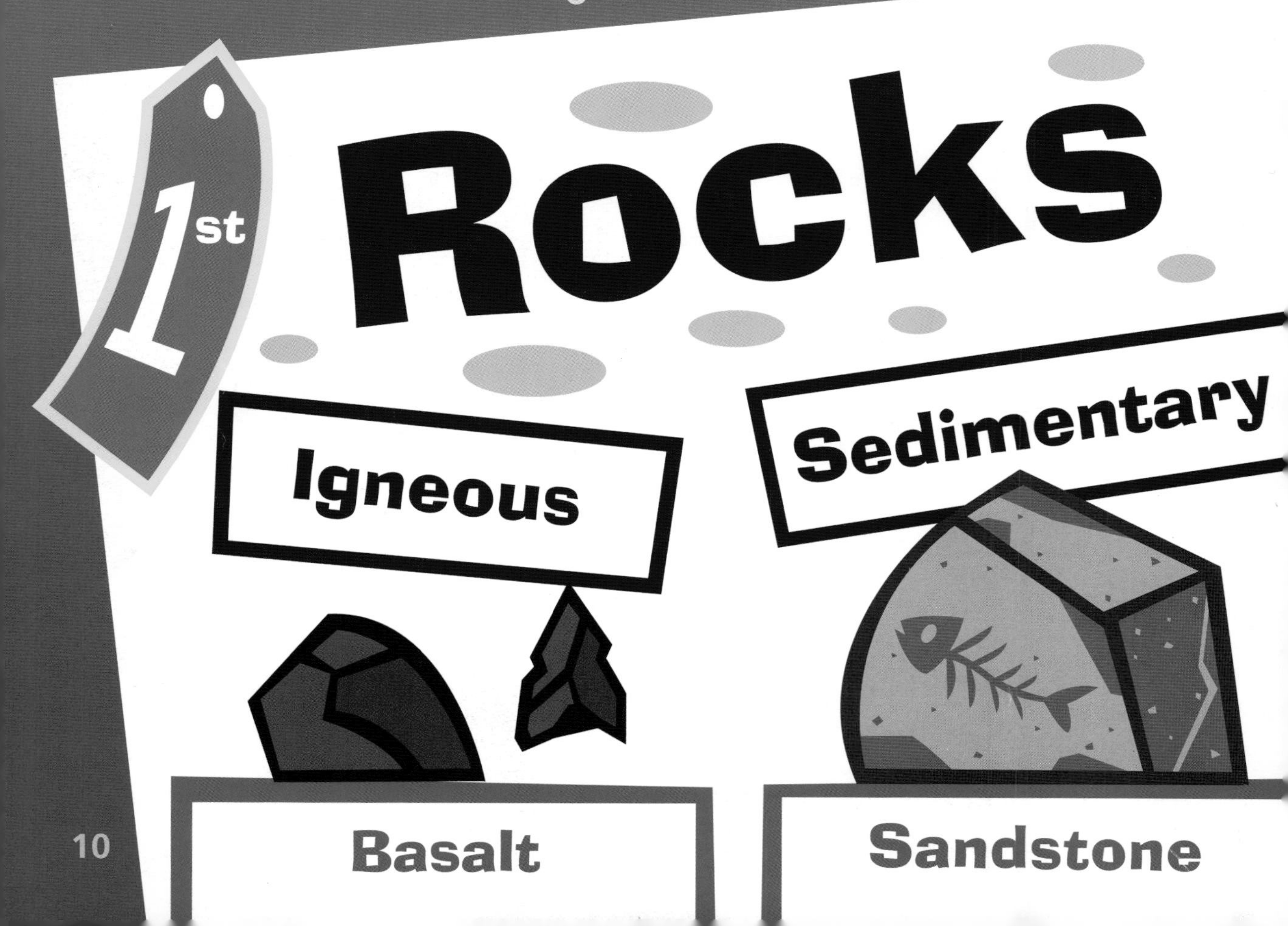

Metamorphic
Marble

Igneous Rocks

Imagine you could dig a hole deep into Earth. You'd find places so hot that even rocks had melted.

The melted rock is called magma. This hot, gooey liquid turns into igneous rocks.

Igneous rocks were the first rocks.
Some igneous rocks are
almost 4 billion years old.

The magma rises through cracks inside the earth. As the magma cools, it hardens.

Sometimes it becomes hard rock while it is still underground.

Sometimes magma shoots out of a volcano as lava. The lava flows across the ground like a red-hot river.

Soon it cools into new rocks.

Sedimentary Rocks

Sedimentary rocks take shape on top of the earth, not inside it.

Wind, water, and ice whip against large rocks. Little by little, the rocks break into tiny pieces. These bits of rock are called sediment.

The sediment piles up on the ground or at the bottom of seas and rivers.

More rocks break away. The layers of sediment build up.

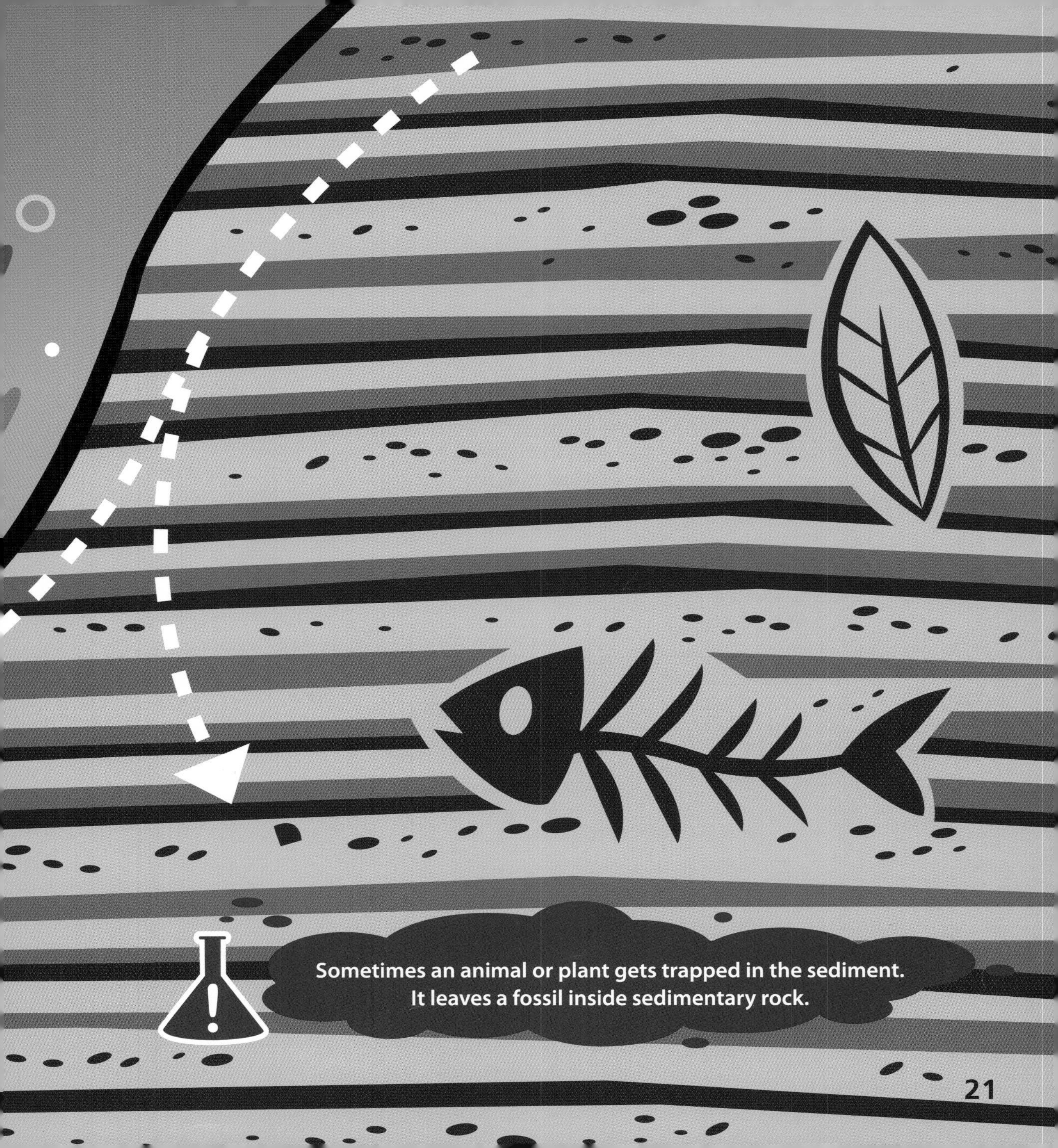

Sometimes an animal or plant gets trapped in the sediment.
It leaves a fossil inside sedimentary rock.

The top layers press on the bottom layers. This glues the sediment together.

After millions of years, the bits of rock have grown into one very large rock.

The Grand Canyon is made of a sedimentary rock called sandstone. Its cliffs have stripes that show the layers of rock. The oldest layers are at the bottom.

Metamorphic Rocks

Old rocks can become new rocks when they get trapped under the ground. Heat inside the earth can change which minerals make up rocks. Or rocks can get squeezed or folded as the earth moves.

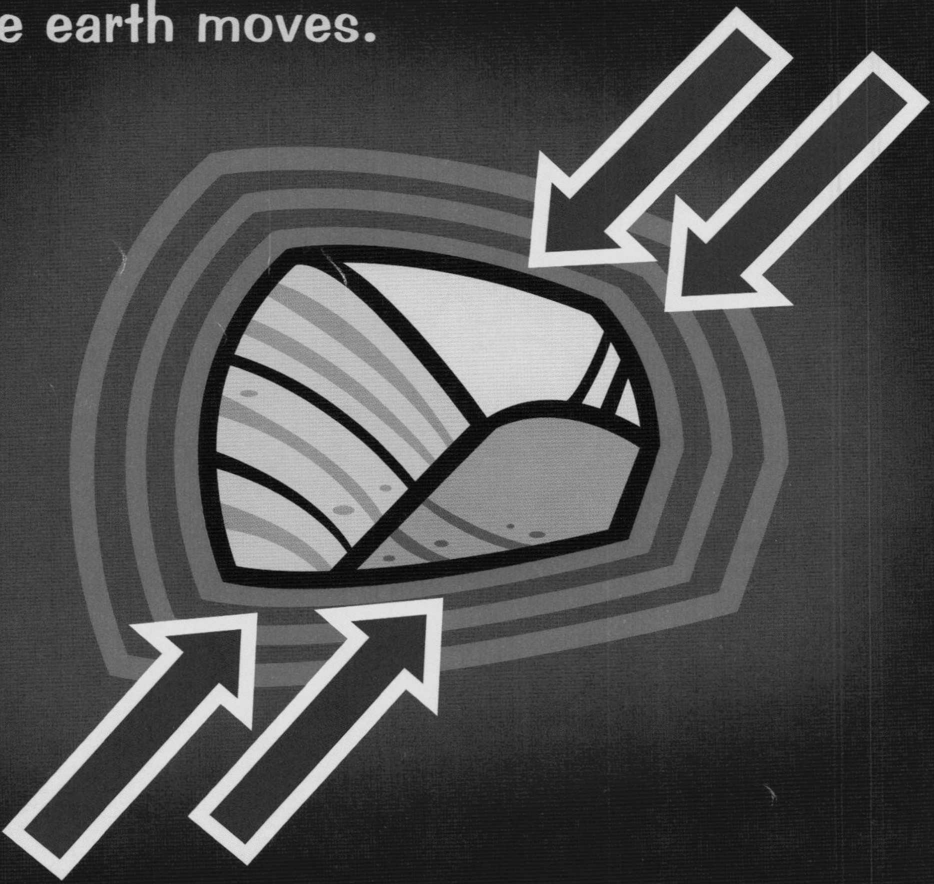

Either way, the new rocks are called metamorphic rocks.

Useful Rocks

All these rocks help people in many ways.

Artists carve statues out of smooth marble. Crushed limestone makes cement for sidewalks. Diamonds and rubies are rocks that sparkle in beautiful jewelry.

Many people enjoy collecting rocks as a hobby. You only need a few simple tools and a guidebook to become a "rock hound."

Look all around. Where do you see rocks in nature? How have people used rocks? You might be surprised to find just how many rocks there are!

Activity

Weighing Rocks

What you need:

Pumice rock (available in the foot care aisle of a drugstore or beauty supply store)

Several rocks a little smaller than the pumice rock (may be collected from outside)

Scale that weighs in ounces or grams, such as a kitchen scale

Paper

Pencil

What to do:

1. Weigh one rock on the scale.
2. Write down the rock's name or description on the paper and the amount it weighs.
3. Repeat steps 1 and 2 with the rest of the rocks.
4. See which rock weighs the most. Is it the biggest rock?

Fun Facts

Grains of sand are really tiny pieces of rock. Soil is mostly made of bits of rock, too.

Did you know that we eat a mineral every day? It's salt. Salt is an important mineral found in sedimentary rocks.

A diamond is the hardest mineral in the world. Gold is another, much softer mineral. The gray "lead" in a pencil is really made of a mineral called graphite.

Pumice is the only rock that can float. This igneous rock formed from lava. The lava cooled so quickly that air became trapped inside the rock. These holes of air make the pumice stone light enough to float.

All rocks are part of the rock cycle. Over billions of years, rocks change into new ones. This happens over and over again.

Scientists called geologists study rocks to find how Earth was formed. They also learn how it has changed over billions of years.

Glossary

igneous (IHG-nee-uhs) rock—rock that forms from cooled magma.

magma—rock that has melted inside the earth.

metamorphic (meh-tuh-MOR-fik) rock—rock that has been changed into a new rock by being heated or squeezed underground.

sediment—a mixture that can be made up of tiny bits of rock as well as the shells of sea animals, plants, and minerals.

sedimentary (seh-duh-MEN-tuh-ree) rock—rock that forms when layers of sediment (usually tiny pieces of rock) build up and get cemented together over time.

On the Web

To learn more about rocks, visit ABDO Publishing Company on the World Wide Web at **www.abdopublishing.com**. Web sites about rocks are featured on our Book Links page. These links are routinely monitored and updated to provide the most current information available.

Index